SCHIRMER'S LIBRARY
OF MUSICAL CLASSICS

Vol. 224

T0071649

Camille Saint-Saëns

Op. 28

Introduction
and
Rondo Capriccioso

For Violin and Piano

Edited and Fingered by
HENRY SCHRADIECK

G. SCHIRMER, Inc.

DISTRIBUTED BY

HAL•LEONARD®
CORPORATION
7777 W. BLUEMOUND RD. P.O. BOX 13819 MILWAUKEE, WI 53213

Introduction
et
Rondo Capriccioso.

Edited and fingered by
Henry Schradieck.

CAMILLE SAINT-SAËNS, Op. 28.

15214

Introduction
et
Rondo Capriccioso.

Edited and fingered by
Henry Schradieck.

Violin.

CAMILLE SAINT-SAËNS, Op. 28.

Andante malinconico. (♩ = 52)

Violin.

Violin.

Violin.

Violin.

Violin.

Violin.

Più allegro. ($\flat$ = 120)

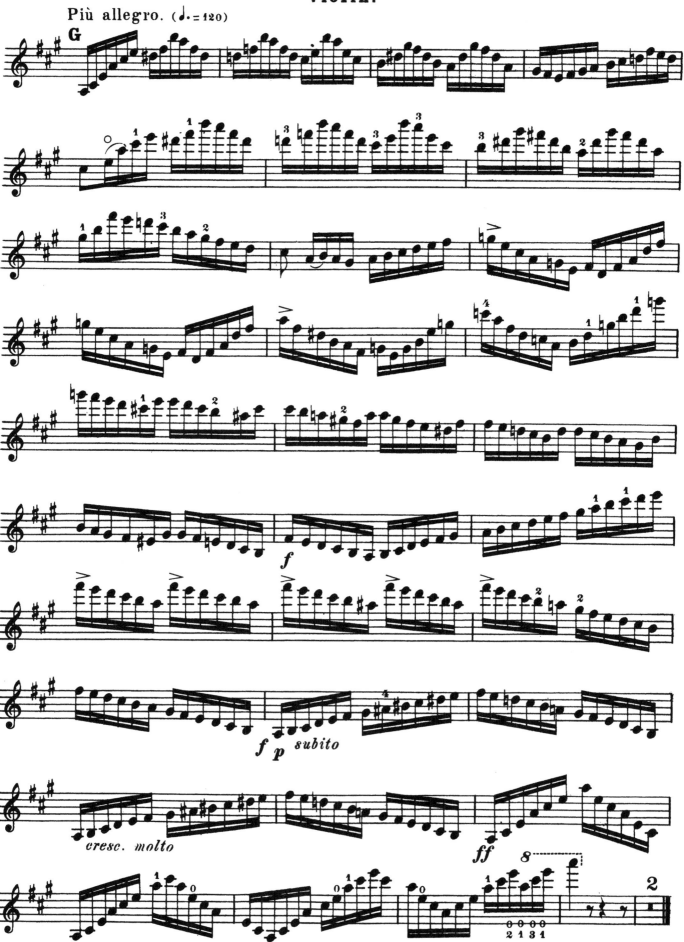

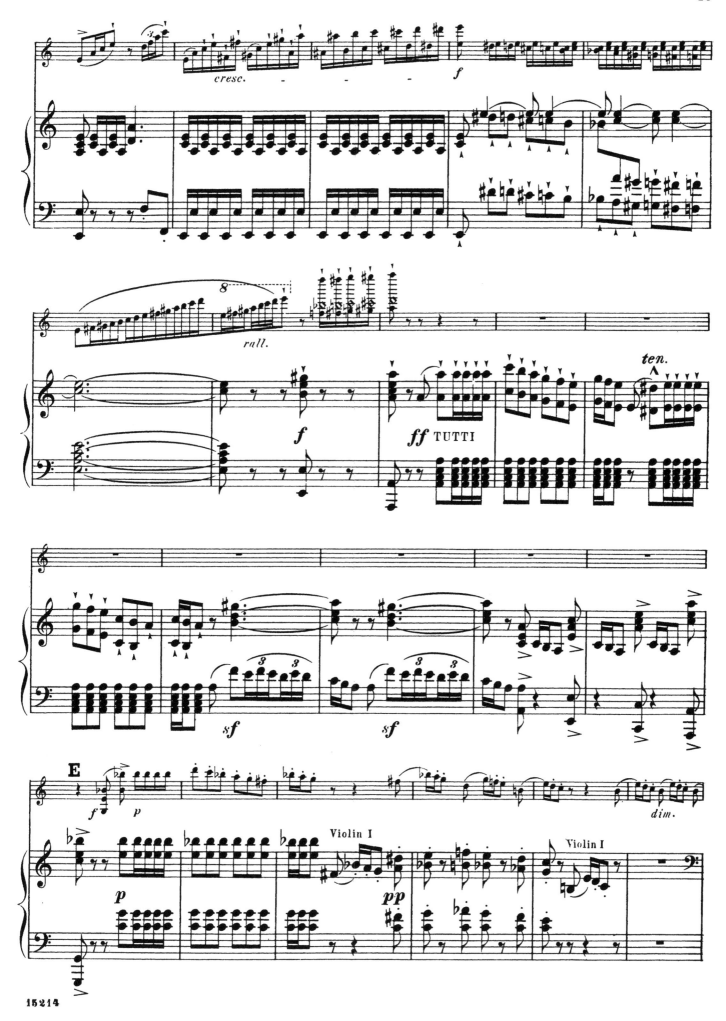

15214

SCHIRMER'S LIBRARY
of Musical Classics
VIOLIN AND PIANO
SERIES ONE

G. SCHIRMER, Inc.

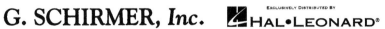

EXCLUSIVELY DISTRIBUTED BY HAL•LEONARD®